Dear

yesterday it was
the hard leading you
    Today He has
anointed you to lead
the way while He walks
with you as His
vanguard.

In Christ's love,
    Greg & Malon

Jesus and the Cross

Pocket Guide

✧ ✧ ✧

William Barclay

Westminster John Knox Press
Louisville, Kentucky

Jesus and the Cross is a selection of readings from
William Barclay's original book *Crucified and Crowned*,
published by SCM Press Limited, 1961.

Designed by
ANDREW MILNE DESIGN

Published in 2001 by
WESTMINSTER JOHN KNOX PRESS
Louisville, Kentucky

Printed in Hong Kong

01 02 03 04 05 06 07 08 09 00 — 10 9 8 7 6 5 4 3 2 1

A catalog card for this book may be obtained from the
Library of Congress.

ISBN 0-664-22347-8

Contents

SUNDAY:
The donkey ride

AN ACT OF SUPREME COURAGE

We are bound to say that Jesus' entry into Jerusalem was an act of supreme courage. There is courage which is born of the impulse of the moment, a courage born at some sudden emergency in which a man has no time to think, and in which he becomes a hero by a kind of instinctive reaction. But there is an even higher courage, the courage of the man who sees with complete clarity the terrible things which lie ahead, and who deliberately, of set purpose and having counted the cost, goes on. That is the highest of all kinds of courage, and that was the courage of Jesus when he entered Jerusalem.

SYMBOLIC ACTION

When Jesus rode into Jerusalem, he used a method of action which many a prophet of Israel had used. The prophets had often used the method of dramatic and symbolic action. Men might refuse to listen, but men could hardly fail to see; and again and again the prophets had cast their message into the form of some vivid action, as if to say: *"If you will not listen, you must see."* When, then, was this message of Jesus?

A CLAIM TO BE KING

It was a deliberately made claim to be king. No doubt Jesus was remembering the prophecy of Zechariah which Matthew cites: *"Behold your king is coming to you ... mounted on an ass"* (*Zechariah 9:9; Matthew 21:5*). It is easy for a Western mind completely to misread this action of Jesus.

A BEAST OF FUN, OR A NOBLE BEAST?

Nowadays in the West the donkey is a beast of caricature and fun; but in the East in the time of Jesus the donkey was a noble beast. In the ancient days Jair, who judged Israel, had thirty sons who rode on thirty donkeys *(Judges 10:4)*. The donkey was a beast on which kings rode when they came in peace; only in war did they ride on horses. The entry of Jesus was the claim to be King.

KING OF PEACE

But at the same time it was the claim to be the King of peace. It was upon the donkey of peace and not on the horse of war that Jesus came. He came deliberately refusing the role of the warrior Messiah and claiming to be the Prince of peace.

> ### JESUS' ENTRY INTO JERUSALEM:
>
> *was an action of supreme courage;*
>
> *it was an assertion of royalty and an offer of love;*
>
> *it was at one and the same time royalty's claim and love's appeal.*

MONDAY:
Cleansing the temple

When Jesus entered Jerusalem, it was natural that the temple should be the first place to which he should go. In the temple Jesus enacted what may well be called the most spectacular event in his whole career.

- ❖ He came into the temple court, and he drove out all those who were selling and buying,
- ❖ he overturned the tables of the money-changers, and the seats of the sellers of victims for the sacrifices *(Matthew 21:12; Mark 11:15; Luke 19:45)*.

UPROAR

It is not difficult to imagine the uproar, the disturbance, the disputing, the haggling, the bargaining, and the swindling which went on in the Court of the Gentiles. Anything less like the approach to the house of God would be difficult to imagine. What should have been what the prophet called *"a house of prayer for all nations"* *(Isaiah 56:7)* had become what Jeremiah called *"a den of robbers"* *(Jeremiah 7:11)*.

THE MIND OF JESUS

In the action of the cleansing of the temple the mind of Jesus is clearly revealed to us.

Jesus acts as nothing less than judge.
Jesus' consciousness of authority is demonstrated for all to

see, in that he was prepared to judge and to condemn those who were responsible for the administration and ordering of what to the Jews was nothing other than the house of God.

Jesus acts as nothing less than Messiah.
It was as if Jesus said: *"The day has come when the house of God shall be purified of those who defile it, for the Messiah has arrived in his own city."*

Jesus acts for social justice.
Jesus' ejection of the money-changers and the sellers of doves demonstrates his passion for social justice. His anger was kindled to a white heat at the sight of simple people cheated, swindled, imposed upon by clever and rapacious scoundrels.

DEEPER CONDEMNATION

There is an even deeper condemnation here; there is the condemnation of anything which hinders ordinary people in their search for God.

JESUS' RUBICON

Like the triumphal entry–only, if possible, more so–the cleansing of the temple was an act of sublime and magnificent courage. It was sheer and utter defiance. It may well be argued that the cleansing of the temple was the Rubicon in the life of Jesus. In this action he burned his boats for ever.

He carried the war into the enemy camp; yet at the same time, by striking such a blow at the vested interests of trade and religion, humanly speaking, Jesus signed his own death-warrant–and he knew it.

TUESDAY:

Concentrated controversy

FOUR DEPUTATIONS

The Tuesday of the last week of Jesus' life was a day of concentrated controversy and teaching. On that day four deputations came to Jesus, each trying to trip and entangle him in his words.

❖ The first demanded to know on what authority he acted as he did *(Matthew 22:23-27)*.

❖ The second sought to inveigle him into making dangerous statements about the paying of the tribute money to Rome *(Matthew 22:15-21)*.

❖ The third was the deputation of the Sadducees who sought to entangle him in questions about the life to come *(Matthew 22:23-33)*.

❖ The fourth demanded that he should tell them which was the greatest commandment *(Matthew 22:34-40)*.

In each case Jesus dealt wisely with his questions and defeated their evil intentions.

THE PARABLE OF THE WICKED TENANTS

There is one parable of that day which is recorded by all three Gospel writers who included parables, the parable of the wicked tenants *(Matthew 21:33-46; Mark 12:1-12; Luke 20:9-18)*.

I Here we find the claim of Jesus.
In this parable Jesus deliberately
removes himself from the succession of
the prophets. He presents himself as the
Son of God, come with God's last
word, God's final invitation, God's
ultimate appeal to Israel.

II Here is the courage of Jesus.
This parable makes it quite clear that
Jesus knew that he was to die. Homer
makes Achilles say, even when death
was certain, *"Nevertheless, I am for going
on."* Jesus knew where his chosen
pathway was leading–and yet he took it.

> ### JESUS' CHALLENGE
>
> *Here in this challenge we see
> Jesus flinging down his
> challenge. His claims to a
> unique relationship to God.
> He claims the right to judge
> and to condemn and to
> reject Israel. He is aware
> that the road he is taking
> will end upon the cross.*

III Here is the threat of Jesus.
The vineyard was to be taken and given to others. Here is
a vivid and pictorial way of saying that Israel was to lose
her place in God's scheme of things, that all her privilege
in the plan of God was to be taken from her.

IV Here is the confidence of Jesus.
The end of the parable is the expression by Jesus of the
confidence of triumph and vindication to come. For that
picture he went to the Psalms. In the Psalms there is the
picture of the stone which the builders rejected but which
in the end became the head of the corner *(Psalm 118:22;
compare with Acts 4:11; 1 Peter 2:4, 7)*. That picture was
originally meant to apply to the nation of Israel, but Jesus
took it to himself to express his own confidence in his
final triumph.

WEDNESDAY:

The anointing of love

The last week of Jesus' life was lived in a blaze of publicity, and in an atmosphere of conflict. But on Wednesday there came an oasis of sweetness in the desert of bitterness, for on that day there came to him one of the loveliest things which happened to him in all the days of his flesh.

Part I

BETHANY

On the Wednesday Jesus did not come into Jerusalem, but remained in the quietness of the village of Bethany. He was invited to a meal by a certain man known as Simon the leper. In Palestine a meal could be a very public occasion and in the warm weather meals were taken outside in the courtyard.

It was at such a meal that Jesus was reclining. Into the courtyard there came a woman who loved Jesus for all that he had done for her soul. Her one desire was to seize this opportunity to demonstrate her love.

PRECIOUS PERFUME

Women in Palestine often carried little phials of highly
concentrated very precious perfume, worn on a chian
around their necks. This woman did the only thing she
could do to show the devotion of her heart; she would
give to Jesus the only precious thing which she possessed.
She poured, not a drop, but the whole of her precious
phial of perfume on his head.

The reaction of the disciples was shocked astonishment
at what they regarded as this fantastic waste. The perfume
could have been sold for enough to buy a meal for more
than five thousand hungry people–and it had been
emptied out on Jesus' head.

THREE ANSWERS

In answer to the words and thoughts of the disciples Jesus
said three things.

 ✤ First, he said that, if a man wished to help the poor,
   opportunities would never be lacking, for did not
   the Scripture say: *"The poor will never cease out of the
   land?"* (Deuteronomy 15:11).
 ✤ Second, he said that the woman had done this
   against the day of his burial. In Palestine the bodies
   of the beloved dead were first bathed, and then
   anointed with perfume. The woman had rendered to
   Jesus the very service which people rendered to the
   bodies of those whom they had loved.
 ✤ Third, Jesus said that the story of this lovely deed
   would go out into all the world, and, so long as the
   gospel story was told, men and women would never
   allow the memory of it to die.

Part II

I Love which delights Jesus

Jesus' anointing tells us a great deal about the Love which delights the heart of Jesus.

First, there is a certain extravagance in love. The alabaster phial of perfume was meant to be used drop by drop; it was mean to last for years, perhaps even for a lifetime; but in a moment of utter devotion the woman poured it on the head of Jesus. Love does not stop to calculate how little it can respectably give.

Second, love knows there are certain moments in life which come and which do not return. There were endless opportunities to help the poor, but, if that woman had not seized that moment to make known her love to Jesus, the opportunity would never have come again.

Third, love puts into the world a fragrance which time cannot obliterate. To this day the story of that woman's devotion moves the heart. A lovely deed is not only a thing of the moment; it leaves something in the world which time cannot take away.

II The mind of Jesus

This story has light to shed on the mind of Jesus.

First, it tells us of his consciousness and his claim. In the Old Testament three kinds of people were anointed.

- ✤ Priests were anointed. The law runs: *"You shall take the anointing oil, and pour it on his head and anoint him" (Exodus 29:7).*
- ✤ Prophets were anointed. God's command to Elijah was to anoint Elisha his successor *(1 Kings 19:16).*
- ✤ Kings were anointed. It is God's command to

Samuel to anoint Saul as king of the people
(1 Samuel 9:16).

Anointing was proper to the priest, the prophet and
the king; and by accepting the action of this woman Jesus
implicitly claimed to be

- ❖ the Prophet who brought to men the word of God,
- ❖ the Priest who built for men the bridge to God,
- ❖ the King who claimed from men a throne within
  their hearts.

Second we see Jesus perfectly aware of his death and the
cross which lay ahead of him. Anointing was given not
only to the living but also to the dead. In the East the
bodies of the dead were anointed and embalmed in
perfumes and sweet-smelling spices. It was that very office,
as Jesus said, that the woman had performed for him.

Third, we see Jesus confident of his ultimate
vindication. It did not occur to him that his work would
be obliterated; already he heard the story of the gospel
echoing down the corridors of time. He who was on his
way to the cross looked forward to a day when all men
would know his name.

The betrayal of love

It is one of the tragic ironies of the gospel narrative that, on the very day on which the woman in Bethany poured out upon Jesus the splendour of her love, Judas Iscariot took steps to arrange his betrayal to the leaders of the Jews *(Matthew 26:14-16; Mark 14:10; Luke 22:3-6).*

Let us try, in so far as we can, to reconstruct the mind and the motives of Judas, using the material which the Fourth Gospel supplies.

I JUDAS WAS THE MAN WHOM JESUS CALLED

From the beginning he was one of the chosen twelve. That basic fact tells us that Judas might have become great in the service of Jesus–but something went wrong. If Jesus was to use a man, that man had to consent to be used. Judas was the man whom Jesus called, and the man who refused to be used in Jesus' way.

II JUDAS WAS THE MAN WHOM JESUS WARNED

John tells us that after the feeding of the five thousand Jesus said: *"Did not I choose you, the twelve–and one of you is a devil?" (John 6:70).* It is quite certain that the rest of the apostles had no suspicion of what was going on in Judas' mind. If they had any such suspicion, they would have dealt with Judas, even with violence. But Jesus knew, and he was telling Judas to s top in time. Judas was the man whom Jesus warned.

III JUDAS WAS THE MAN TO WHOM JESUS APPEALED

There is no doubt that Judas held a leading place in the apostolic company. Jesus appointed Judas their treasurer *(John 12:6).* When Judas left the Upper Room before the last meal was ended, the disciples were not alarmed, for they thought that he had gone out to deal with the practical arrangements which Passover time necessitated *(John 13:29).* Often the best way to strengthen a waverer is to give him some special task to do, and often the best way to secure a man's loyalty is to show him that he is trusted. And Jesus tried that way with Judas.

Still clearer is the appeal at the last meal together. From the story of that meal it is clear that Judas was in special honor. It was to him that Jesus handed the morsel of food called the sop, for it was thus that the host treated his most favored guest *(John 13:26).* Jesus was making appeal after appeal to Judas in the hope of saving him from his self-chosen way of tragic disaster.

Love's memorial

By the Thursday of the last week of his life, time for Jesus was running very short. It was on the Thursday that he ate the last meal in the upper room with the twelve. Out of that meal there has come to the Christian Church that sacrament which is the central act of the Church's worship.

Part I

I The Passover

At the background of the whole meal there lies the Passover. This remains true whether or not the meal itself was actually a Passover feast or not. The whole action take place in the context of the Passover, and with the Passover uppermost in the minds of those who partook of it.

Now the basic idea of the Passover is emancipation, deliverance from the bondage and the slavery of Egypt, and safety through the blood of the Passover lamb, smeared on the doorpost of the houses of the children of

Israel, when the angel of death slew the firstborn in the land of Egypt *(Exodus 12)*. Jesus is, therefore, setting himself before men in terms of emancipation, liberation, redemption, freedom—and that liberation can only be from sin.

Further, he is setting himself before men as the sacrifice for men and women, for it was the sacrificial blood of the slain lamb which preserved the people in the day of the destruction wrought by the wrath of God. First, then, there is the idea of redemption through sacrifice.

II THE COVENANT

The second idea which runs through the whole action is the idea of the covenant. The essence of a covenant is the establishment of a new relationship between God and man on the initiative of God. The old covenant was founded and based on, and was dependent on, obedience to the law. But the covenant of which Jesus speaks is established and maintained by his blood, by his life and his death. That is to say, he is claiming that through him, and through his life and his death, a new relationship between God and man has become possible.

III A RELATIONSHIP OF LOVE

These two ideas become one when we remember that the whole sacrificial system of the Jews had as its one aim and object the restoration of the relationship between God and man which breaches of the law had interrupted. Jesus, therefore, was saying that the sacrifice of his life and his death made possible for ever and for ever a relationship between sinful man and holy God, a relationship apart altogether from law, and therefore a relationship of love.

Part II

I A MEMORIAL

What must his sacrament of the Lord's Supper be to us? It is basic to remember that Jesus was here using the method of symbolic action. He was putting a message into dramatic action, the effect of which was meant to be more vivid than any words.

The Lord's Supper is, then, first and foremost a means of memory. It is the memorial of Jesus. It is meant to act as a stabbing awake of the memory which has become forgetful and lethargic. The human mind forgets; time, as the Greeks said, wipes things out, as if the mind were a slate and time an erasing sponge. So Jesus offered men and women this action which in the beginning set forth his own claim and which for time to come was to remind them of his claim and of his sacrifice.

II A CONFRONTATION

But it is necessary to go beyond that. The bare statement that the Lord's Supper is a memorial and a stimulus to memory carries its own inadequacy upon its face. A memory is necessarily a memory of someone or of something who or which is no longer here, but is gone from sight and from life. But Jesus is not the one who is gone; he is the risen Lord; he is the ever-present one. Therefore, the Lord's Supper must be not only memory; it must be also confrontation.

It is confrontation with the risen Lord. At the Lord's Supper everything is prepared to make that confrontation inevitable and deliberately to invite it. It is the compelling of the forgetful memory and the cold heart to become

vividly aware of that presence which can otherwise be so
easily unrealized and forgotten.

III APPROPRIATION

For us the Lord's Supper is not only confrontation, it must
also be appropriation. In it we must realize the presence of
Jesus Christ and we must appropriate the deliverance, the
emancipation, the redemption he offers us, and so enter
into the new relationship with God. The Lord's Supper is
confrontation with the aim and purpose of the
appropriation of the saving benefits of Jesus Christ.

IV REALIZATION

The Lord's Supper must be realization. It must be the
realization of the terrible, destructive power of sin,

the realization that sin destroys personal relationships,
leads a man to betray his Lord and to deny the one he
loves, and in the end breaks upon a cross the loveliest of
all lives.

Therefore, there is a sense in which the Lord's Supper
is not only the revelation of the love of God in Jesus
Christ, but is also the revelation of the sin of man.

Gethsemane

Gethsemane was little enclosed garden on the
slopes of the slopes of the Mount of Olives, and
some nameless friend must have given Jesus
permission to use it during the Passover week. So out
of the upper rom into the garden Jesus went. From
Jesus' time in the garden certain things unmistakably
emerge.

I IN THE GARDEN WE SEE THE LONELINESS OF JESUS

He took with him Peter, James and John to share his vigil;
but they were so physically exhausted and so emotionally
drained that sleep overcame them. Jesus had to take his
decision alone.

II IN THE GARDEN WE SEE THE MENTAL AGONY OF JESUS

There was the sheer physical side of the matter. No man
wishes to die at thirty-three, least of all to die in the
terrible agony of a cross, for the cross had a lingering
agony such as no other form of execution had. There was
the mental agony of the situation. Humanly speaking, the
mission of Jesus seemed to be drawing to its close in
failure.

III IN THE GARDEN WE SEE JESUS ACCEPTING THE WILL OF GOD

What is all important is the way in which he accepted it.
In Mark's version of the story there is something of
infinite beauty and of infinite value. As Mark tells the
story Jesus said: *"Abba, Father, all things are possible to thee;*

remove this cup from me; yet not what I will, but what thou wilt" (Mark 14:36).

The essence of that whole saying lies in the completely untranslatable word Abba. As Jeremias points out, Jesus' use of the word Abba to God is completely without parallel. That was an address which no one had ever used to God before. Why? Because in Palestine in the time of Jesus Abba, as jaba is today in Arabic, was the word used in the home circle by a very young child to his father. No English translation can be anything other than grotesque; Jesus in that dark and terrible hour spoke to God as a little child speaks to the father whom he trusts and love.

THE ESSENCE OF GETHSEMANE

Here is the essence of Gethsemane. The whole meaning and significance of the words, "Thy will be done," depend on the tone of the voice and the feeling of the heart with which they are spoken. Jesus in Gethsemane is the great example of submission to the will of God, even when that will is a mystery, in the certainty that that will is love.

The arrest

In his arrest the action of Jesus makes certain things quite clear.

I IT IS CLEAR THAT JESUS WENT VOLUNTARILY TO DEATH

It is his own that he could have called on legions of angels to defend him, had he so willed *(Matthew 26:53)*. As John tells the story, those who came to arrest Jesus were themselves so terrified that Jesus actually had to urge them to do their work *(John 18:4-9)*. No man took Jesus' life from him; willingly he laid it down. Jesus was not the victim of God; he was the servant of God.

II THE FULFILMENT OF SCRIPTURE

In all this Jesus saw the fulfilment of Scripture *(Matthew 26:54; Mark 14:49)*. This was not an emergency in which affairs and events had got out of control; this was nothing less than an event to which all history had been pointing. Whatever things look like, God was still in control, and God's redemptive purpose was still being worked out.

III THE PARADOX OF THE CROSS

Luke has something which is basic and fundamental to the thought of the New Testament writers. Luke tells us that Jesus said: *"This is your hour, and the power of darkness"* *(Luke 22:53)*. All through the New Testament there runs the tremendous paradox of the cross. The cross was somehow at one and the same time part of the purpose, the design, the plan of God, and an awful and dreadful crime at the hands of men.

Nowhere does this come out with such absolute clarity as in Peter's sermon at Pentecost. There Peter says: *"This Jesus, being delivered up according to the definite plan and foreknowledge of God, you crucified and killed by the hands of lawless men" (Acts 2:23).* Here is this death of Jesus, in the whole drama of the action of the last days, we see fully displayed the sin of man and the love of God.

IV JESUS IS DESERTED

As the arrest works itself out, as it becomes clear that Jesus would lift no hand to defend himself, there came the tragic end, for in that moment all the disciples *"forsook him and fled" (Matthew 26:56; Mark 14:50).* The end of the road was something which Jesus had to walk alone. There was a part of his work in which no man could help him, and which he had to face in all the loneliness of his soul.

The trial

Part 1

When we put together the material in the four
Gospels we find that within the twelve hours
of the night before his crucifixion Jesus underwent a
trial that fell into six parts, and that he must have
gone through an experience calculated to exhaust a
man's body, to benumb his mind, to drain his
emotions, and to break his spirit, and that yet in fact
he emerged from this terrible ordeal unbroken and
unbowed.

I Before Annas

First Jesus was brought before Annas immediately after his
arrest *(John 18:13, 14)*. At this time Annas was not High
Priest, although some years before he had held office; but
since four of his sons had been, or were to be, High
Priests, and since Caiaphas was his son-in-law, Annas was
very much the power behind the throne.

II Before Caiaphas

Next, during the night, Jesus was taken to the house of
Caiaphas, the actual High Priest, and examined there
*(Matthew 26:57-68; Mark 14:53-65; Luke 22:54, 63-65;
John 18:19-24)*. This must have been, not an official
meeting of the Sanhedrin, but a kind of preliminary
examination, held in order to examine Jesus with a view

to formulating a definite charge on which to bring him before the Sanhedrin proper.

III Before the Sanhedrin

Next, very early in the morning the Sanhedrin proper met in order to carry out the official trial and to arrive at the official condemnation *(Matthew 27:1-2; Mark 15:1; Luke 22:66-71)*. In the days of Jewish independence this would have been the end of the matter, but at this time the Jews were under Roman rule; and the Talmud tells us that *"Forty years before the destruction of the Temple the judgment of capital causes was taken away from Israel."* This necessitated the next step in the trial.

IV Before Pilate

There was the trial before Pilate, the Roman procurator *(Matthew 27:2-26; Mark 15:2-15; Luke 23:1-5, 13-25)*. The was the Roman stage of the trial.

V Before Herod

There was the trial before Herod *(Luke 23:6-12)*. Galilee was not within Pilate's jurisdiction; it was under Herod Antipas, who held his power and enjoyed the courtesy title of king by grace and favor of the Romans. Since Jesus was a Galilean, Pilate sent him to Herod in order to avoid the responsibility of himself giving a verdict; but Herod sent Jesus back to Pilate with no verdict.

VI Before Pilate again

Lastly there was the completion of the trial before Pilate, and the final condemnation.

Part II

All through his trial, certain unmistakable things
stand out about Jesus.

I ABSENCE OF RESENTMENT

From the purely human point of view, the most amazing
fact of all is Jesus' complete absence of resentment. First
from the Jews and then from Pilate he received nothing
but the most glaring and intolerable injustice. The laws of
his own countrymen and the laws of the Romans were
deliberately abrogated to compass his death. In neither
court was there even a pretense of justice. Almost anyone
else in this world would have bitterly resented such
injustice, and would have uttered his resentment in no
uncertain terms. Jesus is the supreme example of serenity
in the face of injustice.

II JESUS DOES NOT APPEAR TO BE ON TRIAL

One of the most extraordinary features of the trial of Jesus
is that nowhere in it does he seem to be on trial. At all
times he is in control of the situation. In the whole
collection of characters there, Jesus alone is in control of
himself and the situation.

The Jews and their leaders are more than half-crazed
with hate; there is in them that which sets a mob on a
lynching expedition. Their emotions were out of control.

Pilate is the very picture of frustration, like an animal
caught in a trap, twisting and turning and quite unable to
find any way of escape.

The last thing that Jesus ever appears to be is on his
defense; rather it is he who stands in judgment.

III JESUS NEVER THOUGHT OF HIMSELF AS A VICTIM

It is clear that all through the trial Jesus never thought of himself as the victim. Even before the trial Jesus had said: *"I lay down my life, that I may take it again. No one takes it from me, but I lay it down of my own accord" (John 10:17-18).*

In this situation Jesus still saw the guiding hand of God. When Pilate sought to remind him that his life was in his hands, Jesus reminded Pilate that he could have possessed no power at all, unless it had been given to him *(John 19:10-11).* Even in the middle of that heart-breaking injustice, it was still the conviction of Jesus that he was not the victim of men but the chosen instrument and Servant of God. The happenings of the last days and hours were to Jesus, not fragments in a set of circumstances which were out of control, but events in a drama, whose course and whose culmination were in the hands of God.

The crucifixion of Jesus

W e look at Jesus on the cross in order to see what that picture tells us simply and non-theologically about him.

Part I

I THE COURAGE OF JESUS

On the cross we see the courage of Jesus. Of all deaths crucifixion is the most terrible. It can involve a man in a death which is a lingering agony.

- ❖ The unnatural position and the tension of the body made every movement a pain.
- ❖ The fact that the nails were driven through those parts of the hands where the nerves and the tendons are, made every movement the most exquisite torture.
- ❖ The wounds of the nails and the weals of the lash

very soon became inflamed and
even gangrenous.

✦ The position of the body
hindered the circulation, and
caused a pain and tension in the
body which is described as more
intolerable than death itself.

✦ The agony of the crucifixion was
the worst kind of agony,
lingering, gradually but inevitably
increasing every moment. And to
all this must be added the
burning thirst which soon began
to torture the victim.

These are not pleasant fact, but this
was crucifixion–and Jesus knew it.

> ### A CHOSEN ROAD
>
> *It is one kind of courage to
> do some gallant action on
> the spur of the moment
> before there is even time to
> think. It is another and a
> far higher kind of courage to
> know that there is agony
> and torture at the end of a
> chosen road, and to go
> steadily on to meet it.*

Two thousand crosses

Crucifixion was by no means an uncommon penalty for
evil-doers and revolutionaries in Palestine. In the unrest
which followed the death of Herod the Great, Varus, the
Roman general, captured Sepphoris in Galilee and lined
the roads of Galilee with no fewer than two thousand
crosses. That was a story that Jesus must have often heard;
he must have known well, and may perhaps even have
seen, the agony of crucifixion.

Jesus knew what crucifixion was like; to the end he
might have escaped from it; yet he went steadily on, and
in the end he even refused the opiate offered in mercy
(Matthew 27:34) that he might endure pain to the
uttermost, and that he might meet death with steady eyes
and with mind unclouded.

Part II

II THE IDENTITY OF JESUS WITH SINNERS

On the cross we see the identity of Jesus with sinners. That is symbolically marked in his crucifixion between two criminals *(Matthew 27:38; Mark 15:27; Luke 23:33; John 19:18)*. It is said of the Suffering Servant in Isaiah: *"They made his grave with the wicked ... He was numbered with the transgressors" (Isaiah 53:9, 12)*. Jesus had always been the friend of tax-collectors and sinners *(Matthew 11:19)*, a friendship which had shocked the orthodox of his day *(Matthew 9:10-13)*. It is symbolic of his whole work that he was crucified between two criminals and identified with sinners in his death.

III THE INVINCIBLE FORGIVENESS OF JESUS

On the cross we see the invincible forgiveness of Jesus.

Even as they drove the nails through him, he prayed:
"Father, forgive them; for they know not what they do" (Luke 23:34). It is as if Jesus said: *"No matter what you do to me, I will still forgive."*

If in Jesus we see the mind of God fully displayed, it means that there are no limits to the love, the grace, the forgiveness of God. We see Jesus on the cross embodying the message of divine forgiveness which he brought to men and women.

IV THE SELFLESSNESS OF JESUS

On the cross we see the selflessness of Jesus. Even in his own agony he remembered the sorrow and the loneliness of Mary, and committed her to the care of the disciple whom he loved *(John 19:26-27)*. Nothing is more extraordinary in the whole story of Jesus than his absolute refusal to use his powers for his own gain, his own profit, his own comfort, or his own safety. He thought never in terms of self, and always in terms of others.

V THE DEPTHS WHICH JESUS PLUMBED

On the cross we see the depths which Jesus plumbed in his complete identification with the human situation. *"My God, my God,"* he said, *"why hast thou forsaken me?" (Matthew 27:46; Mark 15:34).* There are many of Jesus' sayings which are uninventable, but this one is supremely such.

Jesus was beginning to quote Psalm 22. So this saying of Jesus is not so much, as it were, a personal saying, but rather the beginning of the psalm, which Jesus was quoting to himself to remind himself of the servant of God in the ancient times who had begun in shame and humiliation and who had ended in confidence and glory.

Part III

> *There have always been
> some men whose
> kingliness nothing can
> obscure. Jesus was
> supremely and uniquely
> such. Even in the dying
> criminal on the cross the
> robber saw a king.*

VI THE ROYALTY OF JESUS

On the cross we see the royalty of Jesus. Again and again
we are confronted with the fact that at no time did Jesus
seem a broken figure, a victim of circumstances; at all
times he carried himself like a king. It was to this man on
the cross that the crucified criminal appealed as to a king
for a place in his kingdom

Montrose

John Buchan in his biography of Montrose tells how
Montrose was finally captured and brought to Edinburgh
for trial and execution. As the procession passed up the
Canongate the street was lined with crowds, *"the dregs of
the Edinburgh slums, the retainers of the Covenanting lords,
ministers from far and near."* The crowds had been
deliberately incited, and had even been supplied with
ammunition, to stone Montrose as he passed. But the
strange thing was that somehow that day in Edinburgh
not a voice was raised, not a hand was lifted, not a missile
was thrown.

The crowd gazed silent and fascinated on one who was treated as a criminal but who looked like a king. *"It is absolutely certain,"* wrote one who witnessed the scene, *"that he hath overcome more men by his death in Scotland than he would have done, if he had lived. For I never saw a more sweeter carriage in a man in all my life."*

VII The peace of Jesus

On the cross we see the peace of Jesus.

- ❖ He died with the child's good–night prayer upon his lips *(Luke 23:46; Psalm 31:5)*.
- ❖ He died as one laying his head upon a pillow to sleep *(John 19:30)*.
- ❖ He died not like a disappointed man with a broken-heart, but like one well content that he work was done.

VIII The triumph of Jesus

On the cross we see the triumph of Jesus. It is with the cry of victory, *"It is finished,"* that he died *(John 19:30)*. His task was accomplished and his work was done, and already in the astonished centurion the cross had begun its triumphs.

Looking at the cross

Part 1

> **The idea of the work of Jesus as example is deeply rooted in Christian thought.**

1 JESUS OUR EXAMPLE

The simplest view of the work of Jesus Christ is that he lived and died to be our example. *"Christ also suffered for you,"* wrote Peter, *"leaving you an example, that you should follow in his steps" (1 Peter 2:21).*

Hupogrammos

The Greek word for example is hupogrammos, which is the word for the perfect line of copperplate handwriting at the top of the page of a child's writing exercise book, the line which he must copy and which he must seek to reproduce.

Jesus, then, in his life and death left us an example which we must reproduce. Even in so great a passage as *Philippians 2:1-11* in which Paul speaks so lyrically about the self-emptying of Jesus Christ for the sake of men, that self-emptying and that sacrificial obedience are set out as an example of the mind and heart and conduct which should be in the Christian.

CLEMENT

When Clement of Rome was writing to the warring church at Corinth, he quoted *Isaiah 53* at length to show what the Servant of the Lord must be like, and then he went on to say: *"You see, beloved, what is the example which is given to us, for, if the Lord was thus humble-minded, what shall we do, who through him have come under the yoke of his grace?"*

IRENAEUS

Irenaeus speaks of the Christians as

"imitators of his works as well as doers of his words."

POLYCARP

When Polycarp was writing to the Philippians, he spoke about the sufferings of Jesus for humankind, and then he went on to say: *"Let us then be imitators of his endurance, and, if we suffer for his name's sake, let us glorify him. For this is the example which he gave us in himself, and this is what we have believed."*

LACTANTIUS

Lactantius thinks of Jesus as the perfect teacher, teaching not only by precept but by example. The teacher must practice what he teaches and must *"hold out his hand to one who is about to follow him."* *"It is befitting,"* he says, *"that a master and teacher of virtue should most closely resemble man, that by overpowering sin, he may teach man that sin may be overpowered by him."* And if man should answer that the task is impossible, then this Jesus, who was real human flesh and blood, makes the answer: *"See, I myself do it."*

AUGUSTINE

Augustine describes the whole life of Jesus as **"a moral instruction"**, *disciplina morum*.

Part II

II Jesus the Sacrifice

The death of Jesus is the sacrifice which atones for the sin of men and women. There are two general things to be said about this idea.

A universal idea

First, it is the most universal of all ideas. However a man is going to express this, however he is going to work it out, however he going to conceptualize this, he knows that this is in fact what actually happened in the life and the death of Jesus.

Paul spoke of the Son of God who loved him and who gave himself for him *(Galatians 2:20)*, and that is the simplest expression of Jesus as the supreme and availing sacrifice of all humankind. This is not so much one expression of what Jesus did; it is the essential, basic idea behind any possible expression of what Jesus did.

A Jewish idea

Second, it would be next to impossible for a Jew to express his idea of the work of Jesus in any other way. Orthodox Jewish religion was founded on the sacrificial system. It was so founded because it was founded on the law. When God entered into the covenant relationship with Israel, in which he was to be their God and they were to be in a special sense his people, that relationship was founded on the law *(Exodus 24:7)*.

It is the dilemma of the human situation that man cannot perfectly keep the law. Were the matter left there, it would mean that the relationship between God and his

people must be irretrievably broken. But there enters into the matter the whole sacrificial system, whose aim it is by penitence and by sacrifice to atone for breaches of the law, that is, for sin, and so to restore the broken relationship between God and men and women.

JESUS THE BRIDGE

Jesus was supremely and uniquely the one who restored the lost relationship between God and man, whose work bridged the gulf which sin had created between God and man, who made it possible for the sinner to receive forgiveness and to enter into the presence of God.

How else, then, was it possible for a Jew to express the world of Jesus: Jesus to the Jew must be the supreme sacrifice who brings together again man and God, when man and God were separated, and when man was under condemnation, because of sin.

Here is a picture which stands at the very center of all Jewish religion, a picture of the work of Jesus to which the man and the heart instinctively respond, and which the human sprit witnesses to be true.

Part III

III JESUS OUR SUBSTITUTE

The basic idea behind this is that God is King, Law-giver and Judge.

Condemned

Sin is the breaking of God's law, and the consequence and result of sin is to leave man a criminal under judgment at God's judgment-seat. In such a position there is nothing for which man can look except utter condemnation and consequent punishment.

Substitute for sinners

The idea is that Jesus Christ offered himself as a substitute on our behalf and endured the punishment which should have fallen upon us. He is the substitute for sinners; he suffered in our stead.

Suffering Servant

This is the conception which finds such an astonishing foreshadowing in the picture of the Suffering Servant in Isaiah chapter 53. *"He was wounded for our transgressions, he was bruised for our iniquities; upon him was the chastisement which made us whole, and with his stripes we are healed. All we like sheep have gone astray; we have turned every one to his own way; and the Lord has laid on him the iniquity of us all"* (Isaiah 53:5-6).

As David Smith sums up this idea: *"We lay, by reason of our sin both original and actual, under the wrath and curse of God, sentenced to an eternity of torment; and the doom would have been executed upon us had not Christ offered himself in our room and suffered in our stead the stroke of God's wrath, and thus satisfied his justice and appeased his anger."*

David Smith illustrates this by the old children's hymn:

> *He knew how wicked men had been*
> *He knew that God must punish sin;*
> *So out of pity Jesus said He'd bear the punishment instead.*

and by Mrs Cousin's hymn:

> *Jehovah lifted up his rod;*
> *O Christ, it fell on thee!*
> *Thou wast sore stricken of thy God;*
> *There's not one stroke for me.*
> *Thy tears, thy blood,*
> *Beneath it flowed;*
> *Thy bruising healeth me.*

The substitutionary view of the work of Jesus holds definitely and distinctly that Jesus Christ on his cross bore the penalty and the punishment for sin which we should have borne, and that he did so as an act of voluntary and spontaneous and sacrificial love.

The account of the resurrection

Part 1

THE DEATH OF JESUS

It was not long after three o'clock in the afternoon when Jesus died *(Mark 15:34).* The next day was the Sabbath, and the Sabbath began at 6 pm. According to the Jewish law a criminal's body might not remain on its cross over the Sabbath day, and therefore the body of Jesus had to be quickly taken down and quickly disposed of.

JOSEPH OF ARIMATHAEA

Very often the bodies of crucified criminals were simply left to be the prey of the vultures, the carrion crows, and the pariah dogs. But the followers of Jesus had an influential friend who was able to help them to pay what they thought was their last tribute to their dead Master. His name was Joseph of Arimathaea;

- ❖ he was rich and devout;
- ❖ he was a member of the Sanhedrin,
- ❖ and in secret he was a disciple of Jesus.

He went to Pilate and requested the body of Jesus that he might give it decent burial. Pilate was surprised that Jesus had died so soon, but we willing to accede to the request. The tombs of wealthy families in those days were not graves in the ground, but were caves with shelves on which the bodies were laid. Joseph had such a tomb, never hitherto used, in a garden near to Calvary.

NICODEMUS

Nicodemus, John says, came with a gift of spices to embalm the body of Jesus as if it had been the body of a king. So the body of Jesus was wrapped in the graveclothes, which were like long linen bandages wound round and round the body, and then it was laid on one of the shelves of the rock tomb.

GREAT CIRCULAR STONE

Such tombs were not closed with a door, but with a great circular stone like a cartwheel which ran in a groove and which was wheeled up to close the opening. So Jesus was laid in a tomb and the great stone, which one New Testament manuscript, Codex Bezae, says that twenty men could hardly have moved, was rolled up in its groove to close the tomb *(Matthew 27:57-60; Mark 15:42-46; Luke 23:50-55; John 19:38-42).*

THE WOMEN

And the women who had been there at the foot of the cross marked the place where the body of Jesus was laid *(Matthew 27:61; Mark 15:47).*

Part II

THE JEWISH AUTHORITIES

Meanwhile the Jewish authorities had not been idle. Even
after they had seen Jesus die on the cross they were still
uneasy about him. They went to Pilate and asked that
special precautions should be taken, lest the disciples of
Jesus should steal his body and claim that he had risen
from the dead. Pilate agreed that a guard should be posted
and that the stone should be sealed to make things as safe
as they could be made *(Matthew 27:62-66)*.

THE BRIBE

The time was to come when the bewildered guards had
to report that the tomb was empty, and when they were
bribed by the Jewish authorities to say that Jesus' disciples
had stolen his body *(Matthew 28:11-14)*.

SATURDAY

All the Sabbath day, our Saturday, the body of Jesus lay in
the tomb, and the tomb had no visitor, for the Sabbath
day was the day of rest, and to have made even the
journey from the city to the tomb would have been to
break the Sabbath law.

THE FIRST EASTER SUNDAY

Then there came the first day of the week, our Sunday,
the first Easter Sunday. It is little wonder that we cannot
construct an hour-to-hour time-table of what happened
on that day, for its events were so staggering that those
who were involved in them must have for ever looked

back on them with a kind of incredulous amazement. We can only reconstruct the story as well as we are able.

DAWN

With the first streaks of dawn, even when it was still dark, the women came to the tomb to give to the body of Jesus their last loving service.

- ❖ There was Mary Magdalene,
- ❖ there was Mary the mother of James and Joses,
- ❖ there was Joanna, and maybe there were others.

They were worried about the problem of gaining an entry to the tomb, and could not think how they might be able to move the massive stone which guarded the entrance. But, when they reached the tomb, the stone was rolled away, and there was a messenger to tell them that Jesus was risen and had gone before them into Galilee as he had promised that he would do *(Matthew 28:1-7; Mark 16:1-8; Luke 24:1-11).*

As Matthew has it, the risen Jesus himself appeared to them on their way back to the city, and himself repeated the message of the messenger *(Matthew 28:8-10).*

Part III

THE DISCIPLES REFUSED TO BELIEVE

It would only be natural that the women would rush with
the news to the other disciples. Luke tells us that the rest
of the disciples flatly refused to believe the news.

*"Now it was Mary Magdalene and Joanna and Mary the
mother of James and the other women with them who told this to
the apostles; but these words seemed to them as idle tales, and
they did not believe them" Luke 24:10-12.*

HEART-BROKEN

But John goes on to tell us more. John says that Mary
Magdalene hurried to tell the story of the empty tomb to
Peter and to the disciple whom Jesus loved, but at that
time she had not grasped the significance of the empty
tomb, but was heart-broken because she thought that
someone had taken away the body of Jesus.

PETER AND JOHN

Peter and the beloved disciple set out for the garden. The
beloved disciple saw the empty tomb and the grave
clothes lying in it, but he did not go into it.

Then Peter came and went in. *"He saw the linen cloths
lying, and the napkin, which had been on his head, not lying
with the linen cloths but rolled up in a place by itself."* Then
the other disciple also entered the tomb and saw and
believed. *"Then the other disciple, who reached the tomb first,
also went in, and he saw and believed; for as yet they did not
know the scripture, that he must rise from the dead. Then the
disciples went back to their homes" John 20:8-10.*

THE GRAVE CLOTHES AND THE NAPKIN

What was it about the grave clothes and the napkin that was so impressive? There are two possibilities.

I No theft of the body

It may be that the grave clothes and the napkin were so neatly and tidily laid out and folded that it was quite clear that there had been no hurried theft of the but, but that they had been carefully taken off and laid away.

II Were the grave clothes and the napkin lying separately?

It is just possible that the Greek could mean that the linen grave clothes and the head napkin were lying separately, exactly as if the body of Jesus had evaporated out of them and left them lying empty there.

So Peter and the beloved disciple returned to Jerusalem with the dawning certainty that Jesus had risen from the dead.

Part IV

MARY MAGDALENE

From John's Gospel it is clear that Mary Magdalene did not know what was going on. She lingered sorrowfully in the garden, until, in what some one has called the greatest recognition scene in literature, she suddenly recognized Jesus.

"But Mary stood weeping outside the tomb, and as she wept she stooped to look into the tomb; and she saw two angels in white, sitting where the body of Jesus had lain, one at the head and one at the feet. They said to her, 'Woman, why are you weeping?' She said to them, 'Because they have taken away my Lord, and I do not know where they have laid him.' Saying this, she turned round and saw Jesus standing, but she did not know that it was Jesus. Jesus said to her, 'Woman, why are you weeping? Whom do you seek?' Supposing him to be the gardener, she said to him, 'Sir, if you have carried him away, tell me where you have laid him, and I will take him away.' Jesus said to her, 'Mary.' She turned and said to him in Hebrew, 'Rabboni!' (which means Teacher).' John 20:11-16

MORE APPEARANCES OF THE RISEN JESUS

To Peter
There followed on the same day the special appearance of
the risen Jesus to Peter *(Luke 23:34)*. And what must have
been the scene of reconciliation between Jesus and the
disciple who loved him but denied him?

To two friends
There followed still on the same day the appearance of
Jesus to the two friends who were walking the road to
Emmaus *(Luke 24:13-35)*.

To the disciples in the upper room, without Thomas and with Thomas
There were still other appearances of Jesus. He appeared
to his disciples in the upper room, once when Thomas
was absent and refused to believe, and once when Thomas
came back to express his worship and his adoration *(Luke
24;44-49; John 20:24-39)*.

To the disciples on the hill-top
These were all the appearances in Jerusalem; but Matthew
records the appearance of Jesus to his disciples on the hill-
top in Galilee and his commission to them to go to
preach the gospel *(Matthew 28:16-20)*.

To the disciples beside the Sea of Galilee
John tells of the appearance to the disciples as they were
fishing on the seashore of the Sea of Galilee *(John 21)*.

The empty tomb

Attempts to explain away the empty tomb are as old as Christianity itself.

I JESUS SWOONED

It has been suggested that Jesus did not die on the cross but that he swooned, and that in the cool of the tomb he revived, and then succeeded in making his escape from it. He and his disciples then claimed that he had risen from the dead, and he lived on until he died a natural death.

The Gospel narratives make it very clear that Jesus did die on the cross. The Fourth Gospel tells of the spear thrust into his side to make assurance of his death doubly sure *(John 19:34)*. His body was lovingly handled for its anointing and embalming and any sign of lie would certainly have been noticed.

Even if he had only swooned, it is impossible to see how he could have disentangled himself from the long windings of the grave clothes, and how he could have opened the tomb from the inside and escaped.

II THE JEWS TOOK THE BODY

It has been suggested that the Jews took his body away lest the tomb where he had been laid became a martyr's shrine. But it is impossible to see how any Jew could ever have conceived it possible that one who was crucified could ever come to be regarded as a martyr of God, for the Jewish law pronounced its curse on every one who hung upon a tree *(Deuteronomy 21:23)*. And yet this suggestion mut have had some currency in the early days,

for Tertullian with grim humor speaks of the story that
the gardener removed the body of Jesus *"lest his lettuces
should be trampled on by the throng of visitors."*

III THE DISCIPLES REMOVED THE BODY

It has been suggested that the disciples removed the body
of Jesus and then claimed that he had risen from the dead.
That in fact is what Matthew says that the Jews feared
would happen *(27:63-66)*.

It is impossible to think of the disciples preaching the
resurrection faith and dying for the resurrection faith in
the full awareness that the whole thing was a deliberate
falsehood. As Joseph Klausner, himself a great Jew and
scholar, says: *"That is impossible; deliberate imposture is not the
substance out of which the religion of millions of mankind is
created … The nineteen hundred years' faith of millions is not
founded on deception."*

Conclusions about the resurrection

W hat conclusions are we to come to regarding the resurrection of Jesus?

SOMETHING HAPPENED

That something happened is certain beyond all doubt; and the proof that something happened is the existence of the Christian Church. Had the disciples not been convinced that Jesus was not dead, but that he had conquered death and was alive for evermore, there would be no Christian Church today.

FEARFUL DISCIPLES

After the crucifixion we see a company of hopeless, frightened, disappointed men, terrified that they would be involved in the same fate as him who had been their master, and with nothing but the desire to escape back to Galilee and get back to their old jobs and forget. Fear, despair, flight—these were the things which filled the horizon of the disciples after the event of Calvary. This was their condition at the Passover time.

COURAGEOUS DISCIPLES

Seven weeks later Pentecost came and we see these same men filled with a blazing hope and confidence, with a courage which defied the Sanhedrin and the mob alike.

THE ONLY POSSIBLE EXPLANATION

Every effect must have an adequate cause. And the only possible explanation of this astonishing change is that the disciples were firmly convinced that Jesus was alive. Seven weeks before they had been prepared to go way and forget–in which case there would have been no Christian Church. But now they are prepared to take on the impossible task of winning a world for Jesus Christ–and therefore the Church was born. And it all happened because something or some series of things had happened which convinced them that Jesus was still alive.

PETER'S TRANSFORMATION

We have only to contrast the picture of Peter denying his Master in his craven determination to save his own skin *(Mark 14:66-72)* with the picture of this same Peter two months later bidding the Sanhedrin to do its worst *(Acts 4)* to see this astonishing change epitomized; and the cause of that change was the conviction that Jesus had risen from the dead.

THE GOSPEL OF THE RESURRECTION

The book of Acts has justly been called The Gospel of the Resurrection, and there is not a sermon in it in which the resurrection is not at the center of the preacher's message *(Acts 2;24, 32; 3:15, 26; 4:10, 33; 5:30; 10:40; 13;30-34; 17:31)*. The resurrection, as it has been put, had become the star in the firmament of Christianity.

What the risen Christ offered

THE RISEN JESUS AND
THE EVER-LIVING JESUS

The risen Christ and the ever-living Christ are one and the same. To the risen Christ the Church owed its beginning; to the ever-living Christ it owes its continued existence. That is why for the Christian the resurrection is not so much an event in history, not even the greatest event in history, as a reality which has to be appropriated. And we shall find help for this act of personal appropriation, if we look at the resurrection events, simply as the Gospels tell them, along three lines–what the risen Christ offered, where the risen Christ showed himself, and to whom the risen Christ appeared.

When the risen Jesus appeared to his followers, he offered them certain things.

I He offered them a commission

"Go into all the world," he said, *"and preach the gospel to the whole creation" (Mark 16:15). "Go and make disciples of all nations" (Matthew 28:19).* The commission of the risen Jesus si is to go out and to make the kingdom of the world into the kingdom of God.

II He offered them as task

"You shall be my witnesses," he said, *"in Jerusalem and in all Judaea and Samaria and to the end of the earth" (Acts 1:8).* The task of the Christian is to be by word and by life the witness of Jesus.

III He offered them a message

They were to preach repentance and the forgiveness of sins *(Luke 24:47).* They were to awaken men and women to the realization of the depth and urgency of their need, and then they were to pont and lead them to the one in whom that need could be met.

IV He offered them an explanation

He opened the Scriptures to them, and showed them how these Scriptures pointed to himself *(Luke 24:27, 44-46).* Jesus opened the eyes of his people to the meaning of history and to the culmination of history in himself.

V He offered them a promise

"Lo," he said, *"I am with you always, to the close of the age" (Matthew 28:20). "You shall receive power,"* he said, *"when the Holy Spirit has come upon you" (Acts 1:8).* With the commission and the task he gave them the power to carry them out.

Where the risen Christ showed himself

We must now look at the places where the risen Jesus showed himself to men and women.

I He showed himself to men in the garden beside the empty tomb

See *Matthew 28:1-8; Mark 16:1-8; Luke 24:1-9; John 20:1-18.* Beside that same tomb in which they had laid Jesus with broken hearts in the bitterness of death he appeared to them in the new-born radiance of glory. And by his appearing he turned death into victory and the shadows of the night into the joy of the morning.

II He showed himself to them as they traveled on the road

See *Luke 24:13-30.* When he met them, they were traveling in disillusionment; when he left them they were traveling in wonder. The road that led to nowhere became with the risen Jesus the road that led to glory.

III He showed himself to men in the cottage home

See *Luke 24:28-31.* It was in the breaking of bread, not a sacramental service, but in a village house that he was known to them. *"Where two or three are gathered in my name,"* he said, *"there am I in the midst of them"* (Matthew

THE RISEN JESUS BY
HIS APPEARANCES:

*banished the sorrow
of death,
turned every common road
into the road of glory,
sanctified the home,
consecrated work,
and defeated despair.*

18:20). And it has been beautifully
suggested that the two or three are
father, mother and child. The fact of the
risen Jesus turns every common house
into a temple.

IV HE SHOWED HIMSELF ON THE LAKESIDE TO MEN WHO
WERE AT THEIR FISHING

See *John 21.* Not in the temple, not in the synagogue, not
in any so-called holy place or sacred shrine, but in the
day's work he came to them. Because of the risen Christ
all work has become worship.

V HE SHOWED HIMSELF TO MEN IN THE UPPER ROOM

In the upper room the disciples were sitting in sheer
terror and in bleak despair *(Mark 16:14; Luke 24:36-39;
John 20:19-29).* He came when they had lost their
courage and when they had lost their faith, and by his
coming the fear was turned into confidence and the
despair into hope. But one thing is to be noted–they were
waiting together and they were waiting, as we may
assume, in the upper room where they had companied
with Jesus. We are likeliest of all to meet the risen Christ
when we wait in fellowship, and when we wait in some
place which has been consecrated by his presence.

To whom the risen Christ appeared

Part I

I HE APPEARED TO LOVE

The accounts of the crucifixion and of the resurrection may differ in detail in the different Gospels, but in the center of the picture of every one of them stand Mary Magdalene.

- ❖ She was there at the foot of the cross *(Matthew 27:56; Mark 15:40; John 19:25).*
- ❖ She was there when they laid Jesus in the tomb.
- ❖ She was the first to be there on the resurrection morning even before the first steaks of dawn had come *(Matthew 28:1; Mark 16:1; Luke 24:10; John 20:1).*

In Mary Magdalene is personified the love and the devotion of one who owed everything to Jesus, and who knew it. It is of the greatest significance that the first appearance of Jesus was to one whose only claim was love.

II HE APPEARED TO SORROWING PENITENCE

As far as we can work it out, the second appearance of Jesus was to Peter *(Luke 24:24; 1 Corinthians 15:5).* There is no shame in penitence so bitter and so deep in all the New Testament as there was in that moment when Peter after his denial of his Lord flung himself out and wept his heart out. Here is enshrined the precious truth that Jesus makes a personal visit of forgiveness and of reconciliation to every penitent heart.

There are times when a man cannot understand; there are times when life is a dark mystery and when there are problems which are so immense that they defy all solution; there are times when in face of this distracted world the work of Jesus seems failure.

But at the heart of our personal world there still remains this Jesus, if he is still quite unforgettable, if he refuses to be banished from the mind and from the heart, then in the end he comes—and the darkness becomes light.

III HE APPEARED TO BEWILDERED SEEKING

He appeared to the two on the road to Emmaus when they were talking of the things which had happened in Jerusalem, and when they were seeking to find some explanation for the tragedy for which there seemed to be no explanation *(Luke 24:14-21)*.

The whole point of the story is that they were still talking about Jesus. Bewildered they might be, but they could not forget. Shattered their world might be, but somewhere at the heart of it there was still this Jesus.

Part II

IV He appeared to utter despair and to desperate fear

That was the attitude of the disciples in the upper room, when Jesus came back to them *(Luke 24:36-41; John 20:19)*. They had reached the ultimate depths of fear and hopelessness and despair. But, as Neville Talbot put it, *"When you get to the bottom, you find God."* They had reached bottom, but they were still thinking about Jesus. He was somehow still the center of their lives.

V He came to doubt

Jesus appeared specially for the sake of Thomas *(John 20:24-29)*. The doubt of Thomas did not spring from the intellectual superiority which prefers not to commit itself, but from the desperate need and desire to believe. At such a time if a man continues to ask his questions, if he continues his desperate struggle for certainty, the risen Jesus will come back to him.

VI HE APPEARED TO TWO MEN WHO WERE FIGHTING A LAST DITCH BATTLE AGAINST HIM

He appeared to James, one of his brothers who did not believe in hm *(John 7:5; 1 Corinthians 15:7)*; and, above all, he appeared to Paul *(1 Corinthians 15:8; Acts 9:1-9; 22:1-11; 26:1-18)*. There is nothing so very surprising about this. James and especially Paul took Jesus seriously enough to hate him. Against indifference little or nothing can be done; but, if a man disbelieves intensely, there is still the possibility that he may yet believe equally intensely. The man who takes Jesus seriously can never tell when the risen Jesus will at last confront him and break the barriers down.

VII LASTLY, JESUS APPEARED TO THE ASSEMBLED DISCIPLES

See *Acts 1:4-8*. We may ell say that this was his first appearance to his church. When men and women were assembled for worship and for prayer, it is then that the risen Jesus can always appear among them.

FEW BETTER ATTESTED FACTS IN HISTORY

There are few better attested facts in history than the resurrection of Jesus. And what the risen Jesus once did, he still does.

He comes in answer to love;

he comes with forgiveness to the heart in penitence and shame;

he comes to the bewildered yet still seeking mind;

he comes when despair and fear have reached the bottom, and have still not succeeded in forgetting him;

he comes when doubt is agonizing because the need of certainty is so imperative;

he comes to the person who takes him seriously, even if that person hates him;

he comes to his own worshiping people in his own church.

The ascension of Jesus

Part I

An absolute necessity

It must be clear that the ascension was an absolute necessity. It was in the first place necessary that Jesus should remain visibly with his disciples for some time after his resurrection. That was necessary in order that they might be truly and fully convinced that he was alive, that his legacy to them was not, as some one has put it, *"dead and inoperative information"*, but a living presence. It was necessary, as Denny says, that there should be a time in which Jesus instructed his disciples in the Christian meaning of the Old Testament, in the universality of the gospel, and in the promise of the Spirit.

This special time must definitely end

But it is equally clear that it was absolutely necessary that that period should come to an end. Jesus could not go on making personal appearances to his followers, for that would have meant that, tough he truly belonged to the spiritual world, he was still limited to visible, personal appearances. Nor would it have been right that such appearances should become fewer and fewer, and so drift indeterminately and undecidedly to a close.

This special time must definitely end, and not fade out. Some quite definite end to the interim period after the resurrection was necessary; and Denney is right when he calls the ascension *"a point of transition"*.

GLORIFICATION NOT DISSOLUTION

Still further, something which could only be called an ascension had to happen. A.J. Maclean points out that Jesus could not remain for ever visibly with his disciples, that clearly he could not die all over again, and that therefore the end had to come in glorification and not in dissolution. However, we look at this, some terminating event had to happen, and that event is the ascension.

THE ENTHRONEMENT OF JESUS

Still further, the ascension is the enthronement of Jesus. It was, as Denney puts it, his enthroning *"in reality and not in imagination"*. Jesus ascended in order to reign.

- ❖ As Paul has it: *"He must reign until he has put all his enemies under his feet" (1 Corinthians 15:25)*.
- ❖ He was raised *"far above all rule and authority and power and dominion, not only in this age, but in that which is to come" (Ephesians 1:21)*.

Jesus had come to ascend into heaven to begin his universal rule and kingdom and dominion.

Part II

JESUS' VIEW OF THE ASCENSION

So far we have looked at the ascension, as it were, from the point of view of Jesus.

* ❖ For him it was the transition from his ministry on earth to his glory in heaven.
* ❖ It was the end of one stage and the beginning of another.
* ❖ It was his final enthronement after the humiliation of the cross and the triumph of the resurrection.

OUR VIEW OF THE ASCENSION

But there is something in the ascension of infinite preciousness for us also. It is the consistent belief of the New Testament that Jesus ascended to make intercession for us.

* ❖ It is Christ who is at the right hand of God who indeed intercedes for us *(Romans 8:34)*.
* ❖ He always lives to make intercession for us *(Hebrews 7:25)*.
* ❖ He appears in the presence of God on our behalf *(Hebrews 9:24)*.

❖ In him we have an advocate in the presence of God
 (1 John 2:10).
❖ He is the mediator who stands between man and
 God to bring man and God together, and he
 continues that mediating work in the presence of
 God *(Hebrews 8:6; 12:24; 1 Timothy 2:1, 5).*

Jesus ascended, not to end his work for men, but to
continue his work for men, that in this or in any other
world he may still carry on his ministry of intercession
and mediation for men.

Sharing in Jesus' experiences

There remains still one other consequences of the
ascension which it may be that we can only dimly grasp
and understand. It is the great truth of Christianity that
the Christian shares in all the experiences of his Lord. In
the ascension the manhood of Jesus was taken up into the
heavenly places, and, therefore, our manhood will also be
so taken up. As Denney finely says, the ascension is the
proof that manhood is destined for heaven and not for the
grave, that manhood is destined, not for dissolution but for
glory. Here is the answer to the hope which Tennyson
expressed:

> *Thou wilt not leave us in the dust;*
> *Thou madest man, he knows not why;*
> *He thinks he was not made to die;*
> *And Thou has made him; Thou art just.*

It may be that we may think of this in terms of
Charles Wesley's lines:

> *Changed from glory into glory,*
> *Till in heaven we take our place,*
> *Till we cast our crowns before Thee*
> *Lost in wonder, love, and praise.*

Jesus Christ is Lord

When I call Jesus Lord, I ought to mean that he is the absolute and undisputed owner and possessor of my life, and that he is the Master, whose servant and slave I must be all life long.

When I call Jesus Lord, it ought to mean that I think of him as the head of that great family in heaven and in earth of which God is the Father, and of which I through him have become a member.

When I call Jesus Lord, it ought to mean that I think of him as the help of the helpless and the guardian of those who have no other to protect them.

When I call Jesus Lord, it ought to mean that I look on him a having absolute authority over all my life, all my thoughts, all my actions.

When I call Jesus Lord, it ought to mean that he is the King and Emperor to whom I owe and give my constant homage, allegiance and loyalty.

When I call Jesus Lord, it ought to mean that for me he is the Divine One whom I must for ever worship and adore.